It's Only Milk

poems by

Morgan Brajkovich

Finishing Line Press
Georgetown, Kentucky

It's Only Milk

Copyright © 2019 by Morgan Brajkovich
ISBN 978-1-63534-865-1 First Edition
All rights reserved under International and Pan-American Copyright Conventions.
No part of this book may be reproduced in any manner whatsoever without written permission from the publisher, except in the case of brief quotations embodied in critical articles and reviews.

ACKNOWLEDGMENTS

Thank you to everyone that helped make this book a reality, promoted, and endorsed it.

Publisher: Leah Maines
Editor: Christen Kincaid
Cover Art: Megan Brajkovich
Author Photo: Megan Brajkovich
Cover Design: Leah Huete

Printed in the USA on acid-free paper.
Order online: www.finishinglinepress.com
also available on amazon.com

Author inquiries and mail orders:
Finishing Line Press
P. O. Box 1626
Georgetown, Kentucky 40324
U. S. A.

Table of Contents

1	Yes and No
3	Waiting Game
4	2012
5	2015
6	Not So Cold Turkey
8	Where the Sick Go
9	Puddled People
10	She's Drowning
11	How Long is too Long?
12	Ashes Taste Better Wet
14	It Makes Sense Right?
15	Enamored of You
16	No Longer Enamored
18	My Mom Still Thinks it's a Phase
19	Laundry Day
20	It's Fine
21	An Ode to You
22	November 27
23	This Poem is Lack Luster
24	On Being Nothing
25	L is for Lilacs
26	For Lost Girls
27	Bio

Yes and No

Pawn over me like the girls on Sixth Street
Looking for a hit
Just a tip, just a slip, just one more,
Says the girl with Oklahoma smiles and
Alabama breath.

Through the window see 'em struggle
Barely standing, slightly snarling
Darling, sweetheart, where have you gone?
Left yourself in San Jose,
Tried to find your missing teeth
In different states.

Opening up to Channel only
To be locked out of yourself
Unable to get in touch with
The remains under your skin
A sin it is to be this curious
About things found forbidden.

Your sister's hair matches mine
A sweet Christian losing
Her drone-like mind, to
Bigger hands than her man
Florescent being so bright
Only a book has ever seen them.

Backwoods mother
Yelling to the spit falling
From her flapping lips
As she twists up some gin
Fabric starts to bust in hot
Pursuit, tell 'em yes
If you can find your tongue.

Grantville girl finds her place
In the world of no
Tears dig the grave she deserves
Sprinkles pills and bottles
Into dark dirt, watering the sprouts
Hoping to grow a better body
To withstand the toll
Of this messed up humanity.

Waiting Game

When he comes
I want to be with my books
Under collages of my youth
Scattered poems surrounding
My sullen bones and paper skin
Cradling a Marlboro with one
And a pinot in the other

2012

Cloudy water surrounds her legs
Lap it up, unless
You have someone else
To quench that thirst.

Celibacy runs
Around your mouth
While his tongue
Runs down your spine.

It's fine. It's all right.

It's only pen to paper.
It's only natural.

Leaky faucet of a mind
Lapse of unwanted time
Pills, placebo taken
Not mine.

It's fine. It's all right.

2015

Exhaustion rips through this life form
Like the roots of a tree
Breaking bone like concrete

I'm not sure where, but I live here
Under the blankets and all of the sheets
Coil me up in a bed of snakes
Tread lightly, this is hallowed ground

Howling sweet nothings into empty spaces
Drooping eyelids and distorted faces
Swirling together like schools of fish
Deep blues and excruciating reds

Running,
Running on low battery
Please just take it out of me
Lucid dreams of a lioness in slumber
Under the shade of a tree
Feelings of nothing but loathing and envy.

Not So Cold Turkey

Watching her as she sleeps.
Knowing that she dreams
Of only me and my hands,
Before they were shaking.
Admiring her determination,
knowing it isn't enough.
Unable to stifle the thirst,
that chokes my brain,
leaving my veins
tired and drained.

Shivering by that old heater.
It's the middle of summer,
but I swear I can see my breath.
Listening to "Cold Turkey."
Begging for the medicine,
to cure this fever.

It drops. I let it drip.
Holding my corrupt nose,
watching as the blood flows.
Falling to my knees.
Tiny hands grip my teeth.
Spitting it at my feet.
Her roses left in the sink as
rotting flesh begins to stink.

I tell her it's not her fault.
Tell her that I'm sorry.
Tell her not to worry,
I'm just feeling "under the weather".
But she knows me, she knows better.

Our tiny room we call home.
Four putrid walls closing in
All this space being taken.
Getting lost in tall oblivion.
Trying to dig my way out.
Wrapping it tighter and tighter.
Just need the marrow to stop the ache.
I need to clean, clean everything,

One last time.

Where the Sick Go

In this perpetual waiting room,
I sit. Always sitting.
Always waiting.
Give me the diagnosis, Doc.
I can handle it.
Tell me with a straight face.
Lying on someone else's sheets.
In a bed made for wheeling.
With the tiny tubes and the constant,
"Just one more."
"You'll feel a slight prick."
"Good job" they tell me.
(I didn't do anything)

I count the cars outside.
I count the people who pass by.
I count the days as they inevitably slip by.
The buffered floors reflecting,
the sterile stench overwhelming.
My bones are in constant shiver.
Awaiting news to be delivered.

I clink like keys in your pocket
or like change in your purse.
These eggshell walls and all the sick.
Gripping bars with brittle fingers.
Stomach swells as fluids take over.
Hair falls as glands take cover.
Eggplant colored bruises
Covering these worn-out veins.
Looking back to the plasma they lost.
Masked men hang bags of foreign liquid,
While the masses that fill the screen
Scream to be seen, as if living a bad dream.

Puddled People

Grand hands cover your mouth.
During dinner nights,
After dinner fights.

Hold the dessert.
There won't be any,
Not in this house.

Candles burn out as
The truth sneaks through
Cracks in floorboards.

Shattering glass
Rattling utensils
Onto antique tiles.

Where puddled people
Slide or
Puddled people die.

Please
don't cry
It's only milk.

She's Drowning

I'm drowning again.
Can you taste the metal?
In my mouth,
Again.

Heart shaped face, my twin.
Do you hear her cries?
In the background,
My friend.

Swollen limbs, unhinge.
Are you sure I'm okay?
I could swear
This is the end.

How Long is Too Long?

Afraid to look over
For fear my mouth
Might fall open
Allowing me to spit
My chewed-up heart onto the hardwood
I pry my gaze from the grain
And admire her face
Just for a little while
All she knows is the atlas of her body
But I told her it's okay to take detours
To just get lost in me instead
For a little while
I am the corner store everyone stops in
For a quick fix
Just to see someone behind the counter
Or under the covers
I am the layover until she tells her
It's time to board again
But I'm waiting in the other terminal
For a little while longer
Hung up on her like a rope from a ceiling fan
Force of rejection knocking
The chair out from under my feet
But I'll keep dangling here
For a little while

Ashes Taste Better Wet

Spaghetti hair caught in tremendous lies
Sprawled over the passenger side
      Holding swollen breasts   trying to catch escaping breaths.

Sometimes,
Minds think of murder
                        Of deer road side
brains on tires that only squeal apologies
                               or they don't say anything at all.

Wilting beauty fell from her faces
              Her puckered pathologic mouth
pointed high
I was the viewer
Slowly watched the switch
                  go off in her messy head
Changing blue to red.
              Red falling into smiles   saying "honey, blow your nose".

I swear. It was the "it's all planned" and "everyone knows"
                              That held my face under water.
From the driver's side,
I heard teeth knock against words rehearsed
Multiple.
Personalities.
Exposed themselves to my windshield.

The borderline pulled her out   legs first.
My mouth flew open like storm shutters
No words worth escaping.

Wondering how her nose, reminiscing cocaine
               led to a brain begging for belt buckles
                             hanging from shower rails
                                         to parties with poets.
Toothy grins led to "see you later(s)"
White laces strolled up pumice pavement
Curly hair bobbed in calm air
An injustice she does for women

These arms hang onto questions and mislead bones
I swear her shadow was smiling
As she turned the corner.

Shaky fingers lit a stick
Slid into the car that now felt exposed
                           with a smudged windshield filled
                                       with smoke.

It Makes Sense Right?

She only likes her tea
Like dirty tap water.
She drips in when she leaves
Feathers in my mouth.
Keep all the lights off.
When the orange topples over
Know the recipe was meant
For her.

When the blood turns purple
Tell them they took too much
Of us.
They will finally see.
When the pastor comes,
Book first.
Tell him the organs
Are past the paper.
I never knew angels cried
This hard.
With gold heels
Between pulsing thighs.

Enamored of You

Not able to show you how I really feel.
I will just write it on your arm because
I am too afraid to say it out loud.
I am shaking, but your breath is steady
on my neck. While I stare at all the black.

Have been sold on your infectious aura.
Listening to you speak for hours has
become my favorite place. I am still
willing to wait. Teasing me with a taste.
Each time, the pain in my chest grows stronger.

Sweet temptress, you radiate fucking bliss.
But I'll let you destroy me, willingly.
Until then, I'll dream of train rides and warmth.
You sleep beside me; I pretend it's real.

No Longer Enamored

Once sold on infectious auras.
Sweet smiles, foaming to the brim
destroying everything,
running rabid.
Lost among buildings lacking sanction
made of corners, leaking cement.

                        Left tumbling
backwards through emotional grieving.
Barely breathing, choking on thick air,
which bodies are forced to share.
Scrub until the memory bleeds
staining fabric that deserves
nothing less, than the lack of feeling.
Still shaking while that body
remains steady, creating waves
of malice and uncertainty.

But, pathologic is not profound
if it can't remember the utter
of liar's mouths.
Confusing mental with stable,
soft skin and porcelain.
Nothing was real, not even
stories in which
that body grew up in.

Gargling laughter; protruding dishonesty
The façade is cracking, fear for its sanity.
No body can keep up a game for this long
without getting the plays wrong.
Don't read too much into the rumors
etched into the warped walls
surrounding that body.
For they don't read left to right,
only burning edges of scripts
and the innocent.

Hate has never lived in here,
in the space between these breasts.
But if it did, it'd sound as if:
"I once slept beside you
pretending it was real.
Now I sleep alone
pretending I never met you."

My Mom Still Thinks it's a Phase

Cold air on my freckled face
Privileged fruit lack of taste
Fingers sewn together by girls
Braided paradises unfold
She is a forbidden Eve
Toes no longer crave cover
Arms reach out for warmth
Shiver in strawberry moonlight
Chains hang like dog tags
Hair runs up her sweet belly

If you see this face without tears
Know it's as special as this solstice
Childhood comforter, my protector
Hide from the air, hide from her
Stomach makes such complex knots
Keys twist family secrets in cellars
I bang on the doors; beg for my right
To have the fruit, take home Eve
He is supposed to forgive me
So let me be, let me be, let me be.

Laundry Day

Dragging my laundry
like a dead body
into the old, blue building.
A man sits peeling potatoes
in his red chair, not turning.
A familiar form in the corner.
We exchange polite "hello's".
Shoving clothes down shallow holes.

"Out of Order" lines the rows.
Blue liquid pours from shaking hands.
Tired fingers push coins into tired slots.
Mindless drone doing what it's told.
Sitting on an empty white vessel
looking at all of the yellow.
Watching unknown fabric
going in circles.

Light pours through old pane.
Running hands into heat on jeans.
Now, wiping stupidity from hot cheeks.
Sounds of a knife on a cutting board.
Flinching as he peels that flesh,
without permission.

It's Fine

My favorite song is static
Your type is silent

These bones are aching
For someone to break them

Your hands are trembling
Never quite strong enough

An Ode to You

Cigarette under my nose; a balancing act fit for no circus, ever. You come out of the gas station with a smile so loud I have to cover my eyes and ears before you see the weakness explode from the space below my nose and above my chin. I can't tell if it's the fact your found golf hat matches the color of the summer sky or how the humidity in the air makes me feel like I'm going to suffocate. But, in that moment I was okay with being me and you were there, unapologetically you. So, thank you.

November 27

Sipping spores through a straw
I swear it was an accident

Being sick is all I've known
Show me health and I won't know

Branches tap on my window
Whisper for me to jump

Fevers break then broke
Fingers cling then stroke

Triggers follow me to bed
I wash them down with Lambrusco

This Poem is Lack Luster

Comparing juvenile sins with better bets than you
Feelings of loss and frustration, long over due
Those sweet scores no longer for grand pianos
Spoken word, a foreign language for these ears
Loving once means nothing quite compares
To ambivalent, unrequited quiet stares.

On Being Nothing

Left holding an empty stomach
Heaving up nothing but dried up feelings.
Making it out, but not far enough.
Her face still seared into my brain like
a branding that was never asked for.
Twisting knots and heavy breathing,
these insides are fucking bleeding.
Seeing pain and feeling darkness.
I swear I meant it, I'm not like the others.

Monsters still finding their way.
Disguised in such beautiful masks.
Spewing lies all over the ground.
With contagious smiles that slip out
only false truths and twisted ideals.

Fetal position under a metal desk.
Lacking a helmet, left unprotected.
Waiting for the bomb to implode my chest.
Counting purple veins thinking how it
matches this heart break.
How the tiny rectangle vibrates, sending
chills up this exposed spine.
Knowing there's anger waiting
on the other line.

Choking on air that isn't there.
Blacking out and coming to.
Feelings of cold brick on an arching back.
Reminders of ghosts and fairytales.
Like the one who stole the color from her cheeks.
Leaving me begging on my knees
on a dark and cluttered street.

L is for Lilacs

Paper petals line
The insides
Of my mouth

I swallow them
Whole
Before they can wilt

Raw meat
Decays
On the counter

It reminds me
Of you
When you were here

Bacteria eats away
At my stomach
For mistakes I made
When I was younger

People laugh at
Things lacking humor
I wince at the thought
Of it being me.

For Lost Girls

If only beauty was saved instead of it destroying what broken women build on top of mountains of dusty books and notes, flowing down forgotten brooks. Singing the words of sweet Sylvia. She knew the answer before we asked ourselves what to do. How these little poets aspire to cook themselves in ovens; engraving your name on the inside of their newly rose stained cheeks.

I wish to give them some form of joy, but I would only lay out bread and milk just to lock the door behind me, as well. If beauty was salvaged in corners of forgotten rooms, I'd live in your chest. I'd take the space found unnecessary and make it my sanctuary. Surely, I was never ideal, but the love I feel for the things that make a pen move in my hand is completely unattainable. Making the oven's stench almost bearable.

It's Only Milk is **Morgan Brajkovich's** debut poetry chapbook. She has been published frequently in her University's literary magazine, Shoofly and Essence. She has also been published in a local zine, *That Platform Zine,* and had an article published in the *Berks-Mont News*. Brajkovich graduated from Kutztown University of Pennsylvania in 2017 with a BA in Professional Writing with a concentration in Culture and Media with a Literature minor. During her senior year she was the poetry editor of *Shoofly*.

Brajkovich has always immersed herself in reading and writing. She is from Pennsylvania, where she lives with her partner, dog, and two fat cats. She was born with her twin sister, Megan, in 1994. Brajkovich is a lover of all arts, including: film, tv, and photography. In her free time, she likes to make crafts and collage, as well as getting lost on YouTube for hours. She is very much a cancer.

www.ingramcontent.com/pod-product-compliance
Lightning Source LLC
LaVergne TN
LVHW041519070426
835507LV00012B/1683